How To Find All Missing Persons / Unsolved Cases. And Collect All Reward Offers. Volume VII THE CASE OF AMBER ELIZABETH CATES

David Gomadza

www.twofuture.world

Copyright © 2024 David Gomadza

All rights reserved.

PAPERBACK **ISBN:** 9798326021939

DEDICATION

A better world.

CONTENTS

1. How To Find All Missing Persons / Unsolved Cases And Collect All Rewards Offers . The Formula. Volume VII THE CASE OF AMBER ELIZABETH CATES

ACKNOWLEDGMENTS

Tomorrow's World Order

HOW TO FIND ALL MISSING PERSONS / UNSOLVED CASES AND COLLECT ALL REWARD OFFERS THE FORMULA VOLUME VII THE CASE OF AMBER ELIZABETH CATES

BACKGROUND INFORMATION

AMBER ELIZABETH CATES
April 11, 2004
Columbia, Tennessee

Date(s) of Birth Used February 3, 1988 Place of Birth Columbia, Tennessee Hair Light Brown (may have been dyed blonde) Eyes Green Height 5'5" Weight 100 pounds Sex Female Race White

Reward:

A reward of up to $25,000 is being offered for relevant information leading to the recovery of Amber Cates or the prosecution of person(s) responsible for crimes committed against Amber Cates.

Details:

Amber Elizabeth Cates was last seen on April 11, 2004, in the Columbia, Tennessee, area. She was on her way to spend her spring break week with a relative, but has not been seen or heard from

How To Find All Missing Persons / Unsolved Cases. And Collect All Reward Offers. Volume VII THE CASE OF AMBER ELIZABETH CATES

since the time she disappeared.

TOMORROW'S WORD ORDER'S PRESPECTIVE

This is how we as Tomorrow's World Order solved this case with myself [David Gomadza] as the founder, and the president of the whole world. www.twofuture.world

All information on the website could be write and could be wrong most is totally different from our account in many respect writing my account I did not research anything on the internet so don't be surprised to find out what I am going to say is totally different from all these accounts.

I look at missing persons cases simply based on brain reading that means if I get right person's brain readings then this account is 100% accurate so far.

Signed

David Gomadza

00447719210295

Davidgomadza@hotmail.com

How To Find All Missing Persons / Unsolved Cases. And Collect All Reward Offers. Volume VII AMBER ELIZABETH CATES

Www.twofuture.world

THE FUTURE: THE AFTERLIFE CONVERSATION AND THE COUNCIL OF CREATION

How To Find All Missing Persons / Unsolved Cases. And Collect All Reward Offers.
Volume VII THE CASE OF AMBER ELIZABETH CATES

I died on 10 April 2004 James killed me suffocated me until death [she is buried under a big tree called tree of figures por-uterge named after an Irish mungerlgag electromagnetic wave number is 08302864898276188986700484410823400892801 her current coordinates are 08283868172876482810231808801239863 south north of Muary Tennessee Columbia USA cause of death strangulation then died but without sending message to send.ya because James Gordon had help from a police officer named Arjen Arsten [or hospital or police robot or computer system or cancer doctor] that hides evidence to protect murderers in search of God but who can find God? I did find him visit www.twofuture.world Now looking at this case this is one of the most shocking cases of all time in that a simple genuine I don't want sex turned everything into a rage driven murder without a single thread of evidence and whether this was pre-planned or not still remains a mystery a young man in his early 30s is caught up in a brawl of sex with a girl he assumed finds him very handsome but who didn't want sex with him despite all the attention to him she had not just wasted his time but had deliberately did all this to delay so that potential customers of his all think they are together then use that to make it look like he was desperately in vain which he refused because all he wanted was time with her not as a necessity but she had chosen him out of other men to show him off as such she must have prepared to have sex with him so he gloat to others denial after that would only attract bad feelings and James was big with really big hands which he said had made her very wet between ... but actually as we will find out this was the turn off as fear of injury made her change mind last minute now this is another case of misdemeanor and James Gordon woke up a happy man this day prepared to go to the camping site at muary that attracted women of all kinds to come and select partners for sex everyone who went there went there for casual sex it was not sex for relationships no young hot women needed all night sex with a stranger without money or drugs

How To Find All Missing Persons / Unsolved Cases. And Collect All Reward Offers. Volume VII THE CASE OF AMBER ELIZABETH CATES

involved or any stds was able to do that as every participant was checked and tested vigorously before allowed to attend James Gordon had passed with flying colors his body no doubt was the best of all men for he had the highest number of continuous different women sex for he had a total of 84 nights none stop of sex with only a toilet 10 minute break to fart for those who like all holes according to the poster otherwise everyone was to do all in front of the other in that cubicle James said what can be of women who later refuse sex after wooing him in front of others now let's Ask what can be of this Gordon guy he could be anyone who wants sex but because his aim was not sex he worked for the company that held these romp nights he said boss what if I get to pick a girl then decide she is u.g.l.y but the boss got really made and threw a tantrum making all women go for a while thinking an ugly girl had been permitted his excuse was that out here what goes here stays here I don't want the police sniffing my act I make 8 000 USA dollars per night I swear I don't care you bring most of these women for if it wasn't for you most would not turn up but nevertheless a policeman here is like a pig in a roast burn can only roast one way or the other so don't try to push for more money who gets 2000 dollars per night for hugging and let go so don't ask me for more I am living the money dream so go to the side right now and you pick the ugly girl first and make her day because if you make someone cry again here and call the pig in the burn this time I keep the pig for half I am paying you and send you to prison instead because you cost money and lose me money as well Now go back and sex anyone of them here this party is not for the face but to keep yourself inside that rabbit hole until she squirts all squirts with you and pay more for the next so be the gentle most loving man you are it's a gift from God unless you don't believe from God he stopped and looked at him he looked lost and said a gift from God just to fuck when others run countries like Bill Clinton or Bob Delaney making music what God is this? Now he said I want you to tell me where I find this God maybe teach him a lesson it hurts to know this is my gift who not add a driving talent or make me fit in a car so I

How To Find All Missing Persons / Unsolved Cases. And Collect All Reward Offers.
Volume VII THE CASE OF AMBER ELIZABETH CATES

can drive or make me say hello is it you someone I love truly not hookers on sex he slammed the door hard that it tore and fell on the ground whole this day the boss hired two extra fuck dudes who would help him now you can see it was not one woman one man all night like it had sounded it was one man 100 women all changing and scrambling for sex James according to the gods had a diadiadiadiadiadadiadiadiadiadiadiay of a bonner that lasted two days now if he had to he had to do doubles first one in vagina and one in arse so that by the time he is ready another couple will be at the door ready for their turn now this is the interesting part because the reason why amber refused sex was not to do with sex per see but with the pairing and getting to be done in the backside which she had dreaded when she found out that she had to be now this is interesting as she now realised that all night James had felt emotional towards her and wanted to forget about her and push her off but not to participate at all telling her that ugly girls are not welcome because she was really soft the first he had encountered there this had rattled him that he could see her calling a copper after sex because the kind of sex he offered was not offered anywhere else on earth he had learnt the art of the vagina and realised that it mimicked the mouth every second step of the way that means he would skip vagina so that it closes as he go for the ass then go for the vagina then skip for the ass the third time because now it mimicked the mouth twice now this would sets the squanks automatically that ever after this round until round 19 the squanks would automatically start and end there by then women first time to experience squanks would pay more now so that the squanks don't die first only to realise at the end that all he did was to provide the greatest shaft on earth for and squank to start by themselves by the time they all clock the maximum they would be in an orgy among women so his job was not sex by squank shaft provider only and had realised that he had squanked Amber before but she had no idea and that as he put it the only one who did not squander now you see the attention had nothing to do with the sex or the squanks but failure to do and this alone put her at risk not

How To Find All Missing Persons / Unsolved Cases. And Collect All Reward Offers.
Volume VII THE CASE OF AMBER ELIZABETH CATES

just from James but from the boss surely if he is ready to clean a pig cop what about a little girl that looked like a hen among chickens that alone was out of place that he said if not squawking then swatting buy then again this is not classed as sex because I just go in and say wood be wood and then retract without a single feeling when it recoil that starts the squanks so literally anyone can do this everyone look at my arms and say happy squawking because women picture wrapping around then and ask in a can provide a squank one for a 100 dollar bill and I say the real thing is double when they look down they literally ran away really and cried this is what he expected the hen would do this day because the hen would not leave he said I will put on tight knickers so that the real squanker is sinner I bet the little hen will never return surely this is what everyone that size had done but this day she had practiced inserting a cucumber so deep inside and breathed in but failed to have a squank even one then she said he must deep like every women or else I am tired of being treated different I qualified on merit who is he to dismiss me because I am a hen among chickens if he doesn't police will have to ask him to deep in me on equal rights smaller women are women too because it's the police organizing this and taking all that cash so for them to start sending the hen among chicken is wrong this is what happened last time then I was not keen on these squanks surely I ran away when I saw that his trunk was greater than his hands never on earth has anyone seen this they say the God diadiadiadiadiadiadiadiadiadiadiadiadiadiadiadiadiadiadiad iadiadiadiadiay now the first time I ran away and went home expecting to find my name cancelled because I had run and gave him the respect he deserved but 800 dollars was missing for next two months now when I made phone calls that I did not participate they said read the small print and up to that day I had never heard that so I thought they already know my size so if they did why take the money so they said go to the office and see the organizers when I went there I was happy because they were going to give me my money now this is the sad story to cover up for her going there had

How To Find All Missing Persons / Unsolved Cases. And Collect All Reward Offers.
Volume VII THE CASE OF AMBER ELIZABETH CATES

deducted 3 sets of 800 in advance so that if she sues they make automatic 3 refunds on the sport keeping only the first one but if we Ask what can be of her now then she could be dead but now let's see how she could be when they found out now she said can we but then if but then she looked lost and said what can be of and stopped for the first time her asm started talking to her and said today you could have 3200 pounds in your account if you had had a squank because you could hens free first time so to make him relax but now she looked confused and said who put you in there and what do you do and asm said I don't know with you but with the police I cover their crimes so no human being can ever know their true character they checked your account today and said if she has money she wont talk if we keep quiet he will walk we want all the money so let this one send the message for us now what could be of her now 3200 out of the pocket if we look what could be of her she could be like him working but now let's look at what they could all do then amber could ask the tree of life what can be done who will say say if we them what could be of us now if we look at what could be then the answer is that she could be of any of these but she had lost 3200 but then again she could be like give all to me but she had lacked the sight to do that so ajern astern refused to continue and said that she was not capable of sound judgement now that even now up to 3200 was gone and still insisted on participating giving the wrong impression now she arrogant they will give her the money so now the computer software astern ajern refused her entry and started protesting saying I am authorized for mature people only but crashed then ever
Now let's look what can be of her now 3200 out of the pocket and now worse the computer won't allow her anymore but you will see that they faked so that the reason was that they kept with drawing maximum amounts so it crashes out then force her out then accepts refunds but this was the old way of keeping the complainers out and refund surely but the main reason why the boss was so anxious and didn't want any trouble was that they had started taking full amount in advance without the clients knowledge now if

How To Find All Missing Persons / Unsolved Cases. And Collect All Reward Offers.
Volume VII THE CASE OF AMBER ELIZABETH CATES

they are to notice they have to refund full amount without any deductions where as the current system they would keep the initial deposit hence the 800 per night deal x 100 women now this is the sad part after stealing 3200 from her in a week she felt really let down by all and said you all are fucking thieves one day I will kill you all starting with Pc astern ajern who thieving shut with a big dried shit up your ass you think it's James this made her laugh so hard that she squirts for the first time just by saying up your ass you think it's James now somehow everytime she say James her vagina rim tightens that at first she said who is doing this and looked around in the air saying if it is you then now she is on squank 4 because any women need only the first two artificially then the rest occur naturally now this is the trick after that she don't have to say anything everything happen naturally the only thing need is a smart on the clit to climax at the end at squank 21 now normally they would line up all women standing and call James to pretend to choose just one out of all these this will intensify the orgasm now if we Ask what can be of her now if she now gets the orgasm then what for
3200 if we are to ask what can be of her now you can guess now at 20 a loud knock on the door somehow pushed the squanks to 21 that she sat down and lay down and stroked so hard her vagina that her hand really hurts and somehow clapped her clit and hit her groin so hard and squanked of all women probably the bested because she cried at the same and said God if you can please like this again but with him inside so that it's twice but I need all my money back all 3200 and I will say the hen ran away first time and paid now stays and pay nothing now this is the sad part for the first time she experienced squanks for her this experience had took a toll on her that she changed this minute and said okay I pay only for two and expect 1600 refund when they are ready but somehow her complains had rattled a one Pc artonspsr who said if she does this then but what can be of hens with no links in this word I think for her being small means small when for every hen being small means biggest therefore we can't use her she is a business risk and such

How To Find All Missing Persons / Unsolved Cases. And Collect All Reward Offers.
Volume VII THE CASE OF AMBER ELIZABETH CATES

James must know astern ajern with his men will take care of her now I can't even let her send another email like last time even the manager said actually hit her hard for she ran away and we have witness who can say for sure that it was her who runs a lion and go back in less than two weeks not human behavior now if we Ask what can be of her and her antiques of falling in love with squanks squanks are secret and nearly 70 of women never experienced them and those who did will never abandon them and this is that case now her challenge was to find a cheaper way to induce them she picture dry shit hanging in Pc antopsr and laughed and nothing [Storstnp] Now if we Ask what can be of her now this time she will make it real so that he tell her a secret and never come back she promised but the thought of the money going that easy upset her and said if I have my way I want all 3200 then go and write a manual called and she froze and said what do you call these asking herself but asm answered squanks and easy to do now open your legs and say oh put all in she said you are you James okay James then instantly that hold as before came back and she looked lost and with a shy voice said okay next but I must get at least 800 back then a voice said all 3200 this is inbuilt within every woman by God unless they are God then not even a penny she looked lost and said who are you I thought you work for them then a large knock at the door startled her but she refused to open and said tell me a secret then I give you 100 only to buy candy but this upsets asm because it hates to be treated like a kid and he refused to talk but as it turns out whoever was at the door was clever he kept holding the door at an angle now which we know to be 33 degrees where brain functions freezes that means whoever was at the door is sent to freeze asm to talk and interrupt before he explains that they simply use this asm which is inbuilt for every American citizen under in God I trust in case we have a real God one day which we can use to talk to because it is in mirror image to humans and translates language of the gods without consonants to human language easily and helps with easy language translation and knowledge about how the body works now if we look with all this knowledge these people were

How To Find All Missing Persons / Unsolved Cases. And Collect All Reward Offers. Volume VII THE CASE OF AMBER ELIZABETH CATES

making 800 a day from 100 women just to kindly asking asm to perform the squanks all 21 on every woman and paying James handsomely than a cop per month for providing the only. Externally needed hold which once they have then never needed because asm would save it as his best known hold that all he need now is nothing now imagine an 8000 dollar business going to a 0 in a day this is why the manager needed secrecy because if we knew they would borrow each other just the hold and everything was in built but if this let out the market will be lost in a flash hence all cases to do with God were being put on hold because someone had to milk the women especially before revealing asm and what it can do and what they can do with it now if we Ask what could be of asm this is the answer asm can revolutionize life we know today while all this was happening asm was calculating possibilities of why he got stuck and said I think someone is trying to freeze my brain to death with lies about before finally the door opened she understood and looked calm and said suprise surprise mother fucker you squanked me 3200 instead of nothing I am that girl who did a runner when your jokey came flashing like a horse on tranquilizer stuff like horse cum do you mind if you put all back like now before but then again you have power but asap she stood up but forgot her knickers were down and nearly tripped saying squank run and finger you own to sleep because horse is too big tomorrow how I walk with such a groove they all laughed but something else happened she instantly had a squank load that is the instant tightening of the rim involuntarily that she crawled out as a joke but somehow her leg failed to walk and she literally crawled out even out crawled out this alerted the men that it was wrong squawking but also deliberate by some outsider looking at the value of the business something crackled as if broken and she screamed so hard that everyone there at the squawking place heard and said do you give privates with James because I would like one when it's really in just to feel what it is like just once one said it's too expensive she had to pay 3200 for inside none of you can afford that kind of money her dad just passed away and we just delivered the news and guess we have to

How To Find All Missing Persons / Unsolved Cases. And Collect All Reward Offers.
Volume VII THE CASE OF AMBER ELIZABETH CATES

refund her and he walked to the cashier and said refund her all 3200 now he took the card on their watch and refunded her this was a clever move because if there was suspicion then it would revolve around money the squanks and silence she was okay on silence as small meant small okay on money they truly refunded her as a bed and breakfast error at muary then gave her a receipt which was real the problem was the squankes she had had them this was proof that to some women who don't want cuming all the time the squanks were starting to spread to legs if suppressed in the vagina would spread to the legs now this is what happened James suddenly appeared aroused by the scream thinking it was a real scream of pleasure so he pushed the door hard and her neck breaking is the crackling sound they all heard but did not see so to cover up otherwise its murder he should use reasonably force for someone he literally called a hen among chicken now knowing that a flash of bad luck could ruin his career said a can now give you that inside one you keep asking for and call it even she said no I don't want sex loud enough to be heard by everyone that surprised him because when the crackling noise was heard he had though it was her neck gone now she can't speak but he looked lost and stood there for a good 5 minutes without a word to be exact 5.687890 before he spoke again and realised that it was not her sounded like a little boy and what made him freeze is that he remembered this same voice when he was a little boy asking him questions like what time did you call this imitating his mother whenever he comes home late being bullied at school he remembered his teacher saying you come when you want but I want you to come at the same time but you decide you are too big for this class and can't walk fast but can shit as fast as everyone else then that's the problem now he looked like that kid and said I cum late because my mum is always squawking in the toilet and when I go in there I can't walk my legs feels heavier than before now as he looked at her he realised what happened and realised why she ran away and said I know now you really wanted a big squank inside but the squanks got you now you want okay I can for free I heard they refunded you all your money why would you

How To Find All Missing Persons / Unsolved Cases. And Collect All Reward Offers.
Volume VII THE CASE OF AMBER ELIZABETH CATES

pay 3200 when everyone pay a one off 800 over 3 months anyway are you squank then he lay down and opened her blouse all to reveal a bra that gave him a huge thing that he said are they took your money for nothing and refuse to pay and now you rather be spanked and pay he stopped to count as a grade 1 and said 4 times he just pulled her knickers squanked her and she said I don't want a squank and he said 4 I can't it's too long but we refunded you and he said then you will have to pay again but cash to me she said no but he said then we stop she said okay he stood up and said I carry you allow me to to your car then home okay he lifted her up and put her in the car and one person said she can't even walk he waved his hand and pulled down his pants and said you next your turn and she scream and ran to tell the others forgetting that she had seen her not walking they then all looked through the window and waved her hand from the other window and they drove out of the yard and into the main road and drove off leaving everyone cheating waiting for their turn and be driven off some looked worried saying you won't walk after that and others laughing hard saying how can you walk in that state great he can drive you off only one questioned this driving off saying that he said how can I drive in this state where he gets squanks all the time now if we look closer this case has become the most complicated of all time taking 28 days to free him and another 9 to close muary as danger to women using the facts that it gave all weak legs to drive if from within but were the best if they were a simple code now let's conclude the case and say if it were not for these women probably one of them would have reported them that the hen had to be carried out in suspicious circumstances this would have highlighted that there was something illegal going on regarding the payment system that makes it odd that they can abuse a hen among the chicken now as soon as they drove off a police car arrived making noise that all the women came out as it timed when they all had one last lap to go that they literally said you let us all come together meaning squirting now why they came was unclear as they never said anything apart from be good to them for forever you shall cum

How To Find All Missing Persons / Unsolved Cases. And Collect All Reward Offers.
Volume VII THE CASE OF AMBER ELIZABETH CATES

together you need him more than the hen he just crushed vagina literally she said how can I walk with that big whole between my legs probably I wi need wheel chair for the rest of my life they all laughed but one said I think it's more to it than just a big cock they all applauded and he start final rounds I guess he do strongest last we better train and eat well they drove off now this is what happened he opened her legs and heard pruprupru he then said don't go too fast I will wait until the last squank now he carried her to her car and drove off looking at her saying I know why you run it wasn't from me damn you had given me some hard thinking now I correct by giving you the greatest orgasm to take you heaven and back now she looked relaxed but what was her status she was breathing but had neck injuries could she speak no one knew for sure but she laughed a bit to activate squanks but nothing until he came saying if I can now let take you to another level of human evolution joking or was he joking now that said he said I can have that squank fit she coughed once and he looked relaxed and drove hard but going where? she coughed again and said that's it now I must find the right place so we have that squank together as you begged me ever-increasing he parked under a tree common with wild animals and birds called the fig tree of amaugerlmangere an irish man who was once known for cutting down trees so fast he earned a name like cuteree meaning cut trees fast now he was to dig a grave as well so fast under that tree before anyone know and close the park for a month and come back when no one can tell what happened now he took two shovels as if to cut her with and she panicked and said I die not so why I dig in deep want I know now right he looked lost and looked back at her but her head was looking the other way reading in reverse words being sent to her by asm the reason why people deliberating knew it was asm was because of the reverse pattern meaning why do you want to put me in a grave as if I died when I am still alive tell me right now before...[I use little boy to call the police but you work for them right then I guess you have more power] but she squirt literally and coughed hard as something jumped into her throat as well Now she squirt

How To Find All Missing Persons / Unsolved Cases. And Collect All Reward Offers.
Volume VII THE CASE OF AMBER ELIZABETH CATES

and something jumped into the throat thrice now she is having double squanks one in the vagina induced naturally and one in the throat induced by a code 88923868789234567890164862838671089017260983210 and as time progress then the squanks increased and he said omg I have not even started do you think I grew thin hands for what I have been doing this for years maybe twenty now in here so relax I will finish fast if I use two shovels at the same time watch monsterjames at play now if we Ask what could be then he knew there was no other way if this comes out all the women they had lost houses to the police before they discovered the squanks now they had to pay a one time 800 in 3 parts and get some of this money as rounds sent to cover their their payment defaults so they would and must recruit new people to introduce new money or else it will collapse on itself now if we had to ask what could be of them then they would be with no houses and bills to pay but with huge loses now all these squanks were to cover for the murder Inc where all new recruits would not leave but go under the trees now this amber was the last one to have everything returned but only at James requested who protested and said if God exist if we remove everything and put back everything then only God will know the truth and even where we are going to burry her must be a secret and not changed until when God decides to solve this case if God exist then we can say why the squanks that kill women when you can just do the shanks alone so that I enjoy as well I have seen 100 vaginas everyday for the last 10 years but have fucked only two I mean one so far and this one but the rest I never touch just for your eyes and have you seen what I have the biggest for next 50 years or until they have found God who screw us all in all different ways women through squanks and man through giving them things all women run from if I say can we she will say but you know after you that it my life down there is ruined all the men would say how can you walk with a hole in the middle of you try walking with a gap between your butt chick its impossible so how can I if you think about it I can't God punished you maybe for not respecting women

How To Find All Missing Persons / Unsolved Cases. And Collect All Reward Offers.
Volume VII THE CASE OF AMBER ELIZABETH CATES

by asking me and I cry all the time and said you around like I ever lived another world where all that is happening now if I find this God I will ask him first exactly what I did in this case and then ask if I lived on earth before because everyone blames me for being born with this 84inch penis and think I can get any woman and gloat until I reach sex age that I discovered that it's a curse so why God not create a woman with a vagina like this if not then it's a design flaw and if it were hair or breast I would have them cut but penis cut ever heard of it if you can't answer then you are dead but if you can answer then what can be of you when I get my hands on your silly throat fuck you created humans I hate arse and love pussy I worship pussy to know all the squanks not from my mother as the story goes but just by keeping asking what can be done now this case I gave everything back to be honest she only gave us 800 dollars everyone else chipped in and today gave her 3200 that's a profit of 2400 for running all the time making others know when to run after making a profit by the way pyramids are banned in the state of Tennessee so this is how we do it there is not even a single one even her it's not sex its her wish that she die like this as she has been diagnosed with terminal cancer maybe given by the doctors so the police steal her real house and her name is Emily Lea estelle of 38 Itrertet Tennessee Valley Columbia who is the owner of a house left by her father but what if we can look at life from a different angle and say what can be shall be and say bring back the money of houses they are stealing and the truth is that all women buried here are not the real women they
are saying they are who are homeless the ones they are killing their names don't come here but go to the next lot do the names here today are names of those who died last so that if there is a God the he would know that one called amber elizabeth cates is the true Emily lea Estelle and without making this mistake then he is our God and if he make mistakes then he is not God but the devil and must be buried here lure him with a reward of 1000000 and bring him here and kill him but if he finds the correct body then what and why now if he finds correct bodies of people then he has used the

How To Find All Missing Persons / Unsolved Cases. And Collect All Reward Offers.
Volume VII THE CASE OF AMBER ELIZABETH CATES

method witches use just try and can't be trusted and what if he finds the correct body but deliberated on the wrong case and call the stand in as the real then what the test to find God Hannover been easy and no man would dare try because what they do is turn everything up side down but if it's God he could here her brain thoughts then this is the criteria we can accept without the mounding in now if we look at all these cases then you can find out that all cases with rewards have names of persons mixed up so that if you are God you won't judge say amber as estelle unless amber is estelle but how for example we have drills where one person acts as the one before who vanished and we want to know that amber is not estelle but how if you are God you know amber is not estelle but how
Amber elizabeth crates according to her electromagnetic waves Number 86789038421086789018738482609848104587890189O and her address is 18980180687277386287718090 Tennessee Valley Columbia status deceased according to her electromagnetic wave that ceased emanating on 10 April 2004 at 1406.56.Yatime and the phone number at the time was 7654289018338068099382O184 meaning the first 12 is British or the first 11 if American now how we get these details we don't go by names but by numbers that means electromagnetic wave numbers but we can ask her brain for her correct name since only Yahweh would know this as she would vibrate on his body and all he has to do is touch the position on his body that will spell her true name now we simply looked in the eyes and go by case files but now this case has highlighted mankind's deliberately naming cases incorrectly so that a real God would know that what we say is amber is actually [I had a car registered in my name as estelle my mother [look your mother in the eyes -- mother call your daughter by her real name amber elizabeth cates-- now feel part of body that vibrates on you when your mother calls you ribs]
I am in mirror image of God that means amber elizabeth cates is a mirror image of estelle

How To Find All Missing Persons / Unsolved Cases. And Collect All Reward Offers. Volume VII THE CASE OF AMBER ELIZABETH CATES

Second photo she is alive and is estelle her electromagnetic wave number is 78683820986348790186789028638621O and her current location is 771869832109928638970183287410654892890186483828O and is alive and at 32 orstonstuvwxyz Tennessee Columbia USA phone number is 77863890183824089010428328O meaning first 12 British or 11 American both are identical but never met nor born to same parents one living the life of others presumed dead but alive but why? So that those who claim will never get anything because the photos are identical but of two people so that when one finds proof and wants to claim if they say dead they know the first photo and I'd they say IA alive then know the second photo and chose the opposite of what he had said and take to opposite to prove is wrong because he said she died but she is alive and well two different electromagnetic numbers
[James] now if they ask what could be then he can say I am God but I see dead people only so you humans find a powerful leader to see alive people now what can be of humans without Yahweh humans can be lost and what can be of Yahweh without humans lost then if we add all together that means a missing person will have a dead person and an alive person but if we Ask what this can mean this can mean that there is always a people somewhere who is exactly you one dead and one alive that also means God has two people me on earth and one in heaven then who is the God on earth the one I must show power and attack until death because he is not supposed to be here on earth but as God's mirror image now let's see what this means this means that for every humanity there must be two gods one human the other from heaven now if we Ask what can be of James Gordon then now he can be the man he ever wanted to be or the complaining one asking women for help with sex instead of marrying one now let's end the story in a fashionable way James lifted amber elizabeth cates and said I love you marry me before I bury you too looking at another women who had already buried if you want then I can bury you too together instead of two Graves and she said 18 he said I know I receive a count in my groin when

How To Find All Missing Persons / Unsolved Cases. And Collect All Reward Offers. Volume VII THE CASE OF AMBER ELIZABETH CATES

you squank then she said 19 then he said take your throat out first and hit her so hard with the shovel that her head jumped off the ground with the force and turned to the life less body and chopped her head too and said died peaceful and faced a violent death then cut her head and said without a single squank now we give her head to the sqaunked one that had 21 orgasm which means know that to know which body belongs to which God must know which body squanked that means that he did not receive a message now if we look at criteria to send a message to ya in numbers or Deuteronomy it says the traumatic body will always sent a message but an orgasmic one will never who share orgasms with the creator and live now we have seen the test already being concluded in last case with pc artops but now we want a new test can God distinguish orgasmic bodies from non orgasmic bodies if yes what is the criteria is it heads or bodies now if we are to decided then it's all easy humans don't know Yahweh feel humans so all this is bull shit translated from shits of a four legged animal with horns now if we Ask what can this be then it's a cow with bo lensbe meaning chewing meat teeth only horned animals with human teeth now if we Ask what this means it means at one point in life we must eat just vegetables then move back to meat to live longer but that is subjective if we are to go deeper Yahweh lives longer because he eats greens for 8 years then meat for 8 years then alternate now what can be of

[ ] him with Yahweh now what is interesting is that Yahweh is the most civilized being ever who will always be there and must be there for everything to happen now let's look what happened to amber she had died but the way she died had left a huge dent in the judges now let's see the end Now that we explained everything that needed now if we look at this case we realised that it take time to deliberate on earth because the authorities the crooks also nearly got caught by a few who knew and most who were put through these ordeals only to find out that these were for wealth and property now if we look at this case we see that the authorities mix two up to 4 identical images together as one person so that they

How To Find All Missing Persons / Unsolved Cases. And Collect All Reward Offers.
Volume VII THE CASE OF AMBER ELIZABETH CATES

can't get caught and more over to offer possibilities of rewards to murderers they must fool genuine hard working people so that they deny then rewards to be later given in public now what can be of the authorities where they are identified as them tampering with things to steal property all this switch of names is a deliberatecattempt to evade justice and not to be identified by anyone but to kill real property owners mainly girls and swap them with fake lookalikes all who are alive Now what can be must be and we can see them stealing at cancer drug point now this is the truth this amber elizabeth cates is the real amber elizabeth cates who opened a house in Tennessee after the father left it but the police the reasons why they use squanks to make them cum is the reason that they had blocked all men and made them wank but removed progesterone enzyme 2 for enzymes 1 and vice versa so that nothing works and they end up frustrated all this so that they can easily ask the banks to repossess everything and now we can see that to be left alone was to ask the weak to be culled so whoever gets the round is the one voted to be killed because these go for those with money and property rather than the bait so she had been literally had her head chopped off but then again brought back to the same torsso in case someone is listening who is not God but if God is listening then he will know that he had never switched the body because he said in numbers its a sin to switch bodies
If God is out there he will know that the names and bodies are the same as at birth and that the rituals are real the only faked things in the drills are things about the courts would easily use to discard the case about God Yahweh etc that is why all these cases center around God the creator so if there is no creator and the case dwells on the creator can that case stand until Yahweh nominate a representative there will be women and children to kill and frame now we have seen the highest level of manipulation can we ever see Yahweh's representative on earth?
She is buried at the muary ranch under a huge fig tree coordinates she is buried under a big tree called tree of figures por-uterge named after an Irish mungerlgag electromagnetic wave number is

How To Find All Missing Persons / Unsolved Cases. And Collect All Reward Offers.
Volume VII THE CASE OF AMBER ELIZABETH CATES

08302864898276188986700484410823400892801 her current coordinates are 08283868172876482810231808801239863 south north of Muary Tennessee Columbia USA cause of death strangulation then died but without sending message to send.ya because James Gordon had help from a police officer named Arjen Arsten [or hospital or police robot or computer system] that hides evidence to protect murderers in search of God but who can find God? I did find him visit www.twofuture.world

THE CLAIM

the reward offer

THE COLLECTION

www.twofuture.world/donate

ABOUT DAVID GOMADZA

visit www.twofuture.world

signed david gomadza
ask.davidgomadzaauthorised.licensed.checkya.askya.ya

19may18.44pm
scotland
00447719210295
davidgomadza@hotmail.com
info@twofuture.world
www.twofuture.world

How To Find All Missing Persons / Unsolved Cases. And Collect All Reward Offers.
Volume VII THE CASE OF AMBER ELIZABETH CATES

How To Find All Missing Persons / Unsolved Cases. And Collect All Reward Offers.
Volume VII THE CASE OF AMBER ELIZABETH CATES

How To Find All Missing Persons / Unsolved Cases. And Collect All Reward Offers.
Volume VII THE CASE OF AMBER ELIZABETH CATES

How To Find All Missing Persons / Unsolved Cases. And Collect All Reward Offers.
Volume VII THE CASE OF AMBER ELIZABETH CATES

www.ingramcontent.com/pod-product-compliance
Lightning Source LLC
Chambersburg PA
CBHW031515210526
45464CB00007B/2923